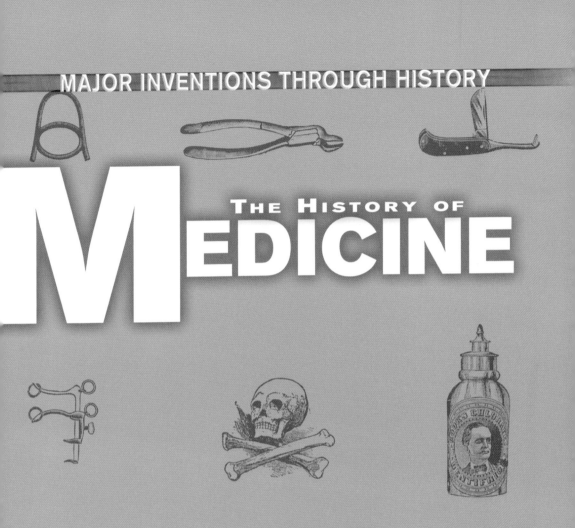

THE HISTORY OF
MEDICINE

Michael Woods and Mary B. Woods

TWENTY-FIRST CENTURY BOOKS

Minneapolis

To the Rockefeller Foundation's Bellagio Study Center in Italy, which helped launch our careers as authors of books for young readers

Twenty-First Century Books
A division of Lerner Publishing Group
241 First Avenue North
Minneapolis, MN 55401 U.S.A.

Website address: www.lernerbooks.com

Library of Congress Cataloging-in-Publication-Data

Woods, Michael, 1946–
    The history of medicine / by Michael and Mary B. Woods.
        p.   cm. — (Major inventions through history)
    Includes bibliographical references and index.
    ISBN-13: 978–0–8225–2636–0 (lib. bdg. : alk. paper)
    ISBN-10: 0–8225–2636–0 (lib. bdg. : alk. paper)
    1. Medicine—History—Juvenile literature. 2. Medical innovations—History—Juvenile literature. I. Woods, Mary B. (MaryBoyle), 1946–
II. Title. III. Series.
    R133.5.W66 2006
    610'.9—dc22   2005013125

Manufactured in the United States of America
1 2 3 4 5 6 – DP – 11 10 09 08 07 06

CONTENTS

Introduction 5

1 Hand Washing. 6

2 Vaccines 12

3 Antibiotics 18

4 Anesthetics 25

5 X-Rays. 32

6 Artificial Limbs 38

Epilogue 44

Timeline 46

Glossary 48

Selected Bibliography 49

Further Reading and Websites 50

Index 53

Introduction

For people born in the years before 1900, life was often short. Many people died before their fortieth birthday. Doctors weren't sure what caused diseases. There were few medicines to prevent or cure diseases. Doctors performed operations with simple knives and few painkillers. Sicknesses that modern medicines can cure easily often killed people in earlier eras.

In modern times, people in some countries can expect to live almost eighty years. People get fewer diseases than they did in earlier centuries. When people do get sick or hurt, they have to endure less pain and they recover sooner. Scientists have discovered substances that can prevent some diseases. They have developed medicines that can treat and cure other diseases.

In this book, we will discover six super inventions that have helped people live longer, healthier, happier lives. You'll read about miracle drugs made from mold. You'll also learn how germs from a cow changed the world. You are about to experience an adventure in the history of medical inventions.

CHAPTER 1

Hand Washing

In 1840 a doctor cleaned an infected cut on a boy's arm. The doctor's hands were filthy with pus and blood from the wound. He wiped his hands on a dirty towel. Then he sewed up a girl's cut leg. Soon the girl's leg also was infected.

What had happened?

Anton van Leeuwenhoek uses a
new invention, the microscope,
and sees germs.

1674

Germs from the boy's arm spread to the doctor's unwashed hands and then to the girl's leg. Germs are microorganisms (tiny living things) that cause diseases. Germs include bacteria and viruses. The doctor in 1840 didn't know about bacteria and viruses. He didn't know he could kill these germs simply by washing his hands.

It's hard to imagine hand washing as an invention. But the realization that hand washing could prevent sickness was actually one of the greatest medical discoveries in history. How great was it? In

GERMS EVERYWHERE

Before the 1900s, most people were used to being dirty. Few people had sinks or showers. To take a bath, people hauled buckets of water from a river or well and then heated the water over a fire. They used bowls and holes in the ground as toilets. Sometimes people dumped human waste outside. When it rained, the waste ran into rivers and lakes. The human waste was full of germs. Many people got sick when they drank germ-filled water.

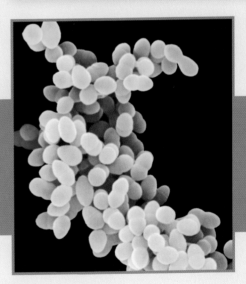

Disease-causing staphylococcus bacteria (staph). As late as the 1800s, many doctors and scientists were unaware of the relationship between bacteria and illness.

Van Leeuwenhoek's discovery goes mostly unnoticed by the scientific and medical communities.

1600s–1800s

Some scientists use microscopes to begin to explore the world of microorganisms.

1800s

2003 the U.S. Centers for Disease Control and Prevention (CDC), a government agency, said that "hand washing is the single most important means of preventing the spread of infection."

Mystery on the Maternity Ward

In Vienna, Austria, a mysterious illness haunted hospitals in the 1840s. Women having babies entered the hospital healthy. But within a few days after giving birth, about 30 percent of the new mothers had died from a disease called puerperal fever. In 1844 Ignaz Semmelweis, a doctor at the hospital, discovered the cause. He noticed that women treated by doctors who washed their hands stayed healthy. Other women often got puerperal fever. Semmelweis realized that doctors were spreading the disease on their unwashed hands. In 1847 he ordered doctors at the hospital to wash their hands before touching patients. Deaths from puerperal fever fell to less than 11 percent.

Despite Dr. Semmelweis's discovery, doctors at other hospitals did not want to wash their hands.

FAST FACT

Anton van Leeuwenhoek, a Dutch scientist, was the first person to identify germs. In the 1670s, he improved on the microscope, a new invention at the time. Microscopes are machines that make tiny objects look bigger. Leeuwenhoek's microscope could enlarge images up to 270 times their original size. He used his microscope to look at bacteria and other tiny life-forms.

Ignaz Semmelweis discovers that hand washing prevents the spread of infection.

1844

Semmelweis's hand washing policy for medical staff dramatically reduces death from infections.

1847

They thought that damp air caused diseases. They didn't know about germs, and they couldn't imagine how dirty hands could make people sick. Many doctors made fun of Dr. Semmelweis's idea.

Putting Ideas into Action

Starting in the 1860s, scientists began to learn more about germs. Louis Pasteur, a French scientist,

HYGIENE: A NOVEL IDEA

Cleanliness improved in the 1900s. In the United States and many other nations, people began to install toilets, showers, and sinks in their homes. Cities built sewer systems to carry away human waste. They built networks of pipes to bring pure drinking water to every home. Cities and states opened public health departments. These government agencies taught people how to keep clean and avoid germs. In modern times, we can buy dozens of different kinds of soap and other products that help us keep clean.

Louis Pasteur in his lab

Louis Pasteur studies bacteria and their relationship to infection, forming the "germ theory" of disease.

1860s

DID YOU KNOW?

Germs get on people's hands in different ways. Always wash your hands: after using the bathroom; after blowing your nose, sneezing, or coughing; before eating or touching food; after touching uncooked meat; after changing a diaper; after touching money; after playing with pets—especially iguanas, turtles, and snakes; before touching your mouth, eyes, or nose.

studied bacteria. He learned that some bacteria cause diseases. Robert Koch, a German scientist, proved that specific bacteria cause specific diseases. Joseph Lister, a Scottish doctor, invented an antiseptic, a liquid that kills bacteria.

Doctors weren't laughing anymore. Convinced by the work of Pasteur, Koch, and Lister, they began to use antiseptic on their hands and surgical instruments. They made sure to wash their hands before treating patients. Because of these changes, fewer patients got infections after surgery. But doctors still didn't wear sterile masks, gowns, and gloves.

Joseph Lister

Joseph Lister invents antiseptic. The liquid kills bacteria on contact.

1860s

Building on Pasteur's germ theory of disease, Robert Koch further proves that specific bacteria cause specific diseases.

1882

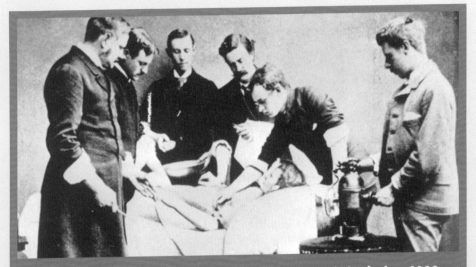

Surgeons and students perform surgery using antiseptic in the late 1800s. The man at the far right operates a mister, which sprays a fine mist of antiseptic on the patient and throughout the surgical area.

Modern-day operating rooms are super clean. Doctors scrub their hands for many minutes before operating on patients. They use special machines to sterilize their surgical tools and equipment. And they wear sterile clothing, masks, and rubber gloves. Dentists and other health-care professionals also wash their hands and use clean equipment and clothing when treating patients.

Pasteur and Koch prove germ theory. Doctors use antiseptic to sterilize their hands and surgical areas.

Doctors and other health-care givers scrub their hands and use sterilized equipment and clothing when treating patients.

late 1800s   **1900s-present**

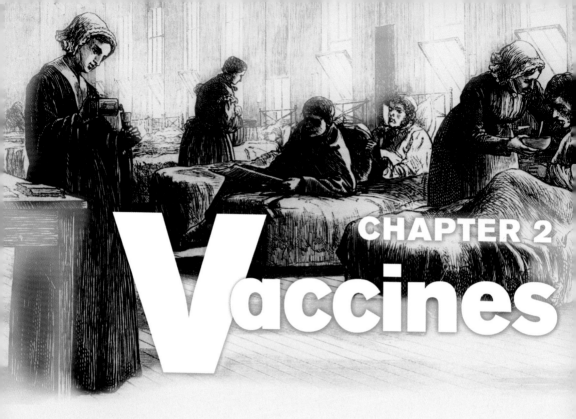

CHAPTER 2
Vaccines

Hundreds of years ago, many people caught a disease called smallpox. Smallpox was caused by a virus, a type of germ. People who got the disease developed big, pus-filled sores all over their bodies. Many of these people died. Those lucky enough to survive the disease were left with deep scars, or pockmarks, on their faces.

But in Europe, people noticed that milkmaids never got smallpox. Milkmaids were women who milked cows for a living. Their faces were always smooth and clear, without any pockmarks. Scientists

The first smallpox epidemic
is recorded in Egypt.
1350 B.C.

thought that milkmaids escaped smallpox because they caught a milder form of the disease from cows. That milder disease was cowpox, which made people only slightly sick. Scientists thought that cowpox gave people immunity to (protection from) smallpox.

In 1796 a British physician named Edward Jenner decided to test this theory. He infected a boy, James Phipps, with pus from the hand of a milkmaid who had cowpox.

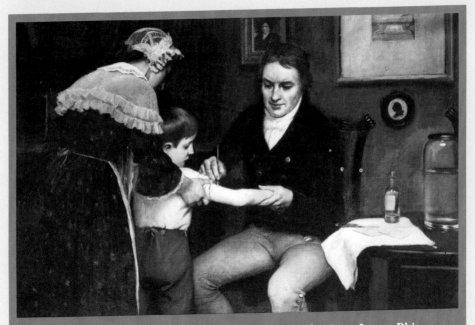

In this painting, Dr. Edward Jenner *(sitting, right)* infects James Phipps *(center)* with cowpox pus on May 14, 1796. Jenner hoped the vaccination would prevent Phipps from catching the more deadly smallpox.

Smallpox spreads to
Europe, causing massive
epidemics of the disease.

Edward Jenner tests
his smallpox vaccine on
James Phipps.

A.D. 600s

1796

James then developed cowpox. A month and a half later, Jenner infected James with pus from someone who had smallpox. But James didn't get smallpox. The cowpox injection had prepared his body to fight off smallpox in the future. Jenner had created the first vaccine—an injection of dead or living germs that increases immunity to more dangerous germs.

This British cartoon from 1802 shows Dr. Jenner *(standing, left center)* vaccinating people with cowpox. With cows growing from the characters, the cartoon shows people's fear of vaccinations.

Jenner's smallpox vaccine is successful, but many people fear awful side effects.

late 1790s

A U.S. government poster from the 1940s urges parents to have their children vaccinated against smallpox.

A Shot in the Arm

Gradually, other doctors began to use Jenner's invention. In the 1850s, countries in Europe passed laws requiring everyone to be vaccinated against smallpox. The United States passed a similar law in the early 1900s. The smallpox vaccine was administered with a shot—an injection using a needle.

Scientists developed vaccines for other diseases, including anthrax, cholera, tuberculosis (TB), and rabies. Governments in some countries passed laws requiring everyone to get vaccinations for these and other diseases. Vaccinations saved many lives and helped keep people healthy.

Countries in Europe require all citizens to be vaccinated against smallpox.

1850s

Pasteur discovers a vaccination for rabies. Other vaccinations also are being developed at this time.

1856

Dr. Jonas Salk

FAST FACT

The U.S. Centers for Disease Control and Prevention made a list of the ten greatest health inventions of the 1900s. Vaccination was number one on the CDC list.

A Landmark Vaccine

Polio was a dreaded disease in earlier eras. Caused by a virus, the disease often damages its victims' legs. Some victims become paralyzed, or unable to move parts of their bodies. Polio often strikes children. In the United States in the mid-1900s, people were especially fearful of polio in summer, when many children went swimming, because the polio virus can spread through unclean water. U.S. president Franklin D. Roosevelt, who held office in the 1930s and 1940s, had polio. He couldn't walk without the help of a cane or leg braces. He often used a wheelchair.

Jonas Salk, a U.S. scientist, invented the first polio vaccine in 1954. Albert Sabin, another American, invented a second, more effective polio vaccine in 1957. The polio vaccine wiped

Jonas Salk develops the first vaccine for polio.
1954

out polio in the United States and most other countries.

Vaccination Worldwide

Although vaccines eliminated many diseases in the United States and other well-off nations, people in many poor countries could not afford vaccines for smallpox and other diseases. In the 1900s, smallpox killed a total of about 500 million people around the world.

In the 1970s, the United Nations started giving free smallpox vaccinations in poor countries. The program was a success. It had entirely wiped out smallpox by 1980. In the early 2000s, the smallpox virus exists only in scientific laboratories.

FUTURE VACCINES: BITE ME

Getting vaccinated usually involves a little ouch! Most vaccines are injected with a sharp needle—and that hurts. But scientists are working on creating vaccines you can eat. Scientists want to grow special genetically engineered plants (plants with altered genes) that contain vaccines. With this invention, people could get vaccines in a bite of banana or a forkful of rice. This kind of vaccine could improve vaccination programs in poor countries. Vaccine-containing plants could be grown right where they're needed. Scientists think edible vaccines might also work better than injected vaccines.

In modern times, scientists have vaccines for twenty-one diseases. Doctors vaccinate babies for mumps, measles, and other illnesses. Many children and adults get yearly vaccines for influenza (the flu). Scientists hope to develop more vaccines in the future.

An extensive global vaccination program wipes out smallpox in the human population.

1980

CHAPTER 3
Antibiotics

Have you ever taken a miracle drug? If you've ever had an antibiotic, the answer is yes. Many children take antibiotics for ear infections and sore throats. If you've ever had a dangerous infection, an antibiotic may have saved your life.

Antibiotics are chemicals that stop bacteria from growing inside the body. By stopping the growth of bacteria, antibiotics can stop infections and cure diseases. In modern times, antibiotics are common, inexpensive medicines. People usually take them in pill form. Even though they might look simple, antibiotics are wonder drugs. They are also one of the most important inventions in medical history.

Searching for Magic Bullets

People have always used medicines to treat illness and injury. Thousands of years ago in ancient Egypt, people smeared a paste of honey and animal fat on cuts and wounds. Native Americans applied mold and other kinds of fungus to their wounds. Some of these treatments worked, but people didn't know why. Some people thought the treatments were magic, driving away evil spirits that caused illness.

> ## What's in a Name
> The term *antibiotic* comes from two Greek words: *anti*, which means "against," and *bio*, which means "life." The name refers to antibiotics' ability to kill living bacteria.

In the late 1800s, scientists learned that germs caused many diseases. Scientists started searching for medicines to kill those germs. In 1928 Alexander Fleming, a Scottish scientist, was growing some staphylococcus bacteria in his laboratory. This kind of bacteria causes serious infections.

Fleming noticed something odd on a plate where some staph was growing. A mold had also started to grow on the plate. Much

Alexander Fleming discovers a mold that can kill bacteria— the first antibiotic.

1928

FAST FACT

Antibiotics can kill only bacteria, one kind of germ. They are not effective against viruses, another kind of germ.

to Fleming's surprise, the staph around the mold had died. Fleming realized that the mold, *Penicillium notatum*, released a liquid that killed bacteria. He had discovered the first antibiotic. Fleming named the new drug penicillin. Doctors used it to treat scarlet fever, pneumonia, and other diseases caused by bacteria.

But the penicillin mold grew slowly, and it took a large amount of mold to make even a small amount of medicine. By 1939 the need for penicillin was urgent. World War II (1939–1945) had

Dr. Alexander Fleming observes the effects of *Penicillium notatum* (penicillin) on bacteria in a petri dish in the late 1920s.

started in Europe. Thousands of soldiers were dying from infected wounds. In 1941 scientists invented a way to make big batches of penicillin.

The new drug saved many lives, especially on World War II battlefields. Penicillin was truly a wonder drug. Doctors called it a magic bullet because it cured serious illnesses without causing major side effects, unless a person was allergic to it.

Miracle Drugs versus Super Bugs

In the second half of the 1900s, scientists discovered many more antibiotics. Doctors needed different kinds of antibiotics because antibiotics don't all work the same. Penicillin, for instance, works on some infections but not others. Doctors needed different antibiotics for different diseases.

In addition, antibiotics can slowly lose their effectiveness against germs. Over time, germs can change their genetic form

MEDICINE FROM DIRT

With the discovery of penicillin, scientists started to look for other molds that could produce antibiotics. Many molds live in the soil. So scientists collected and checked soil samples. They succeeded in finding other molds that produced antibiotics.

One of these molds, streptomyces, saves millions of lives each year. It was the first treatment for tuberculosis, a serious lung disease. Selman Waksman, a U.S. scientist, discovered the antibiotic streptomycin in 1943. Scientists still search the dirt for new antibiotics. They also make new antibiotics from chemicals in the laboratory.

Scientists learn to make large amounts of penicillin, saving the lives of many soldiers fighting in World War II.

1941

Selman Waksman discovers streptomycin, a treatment for tuberculosis.

1943

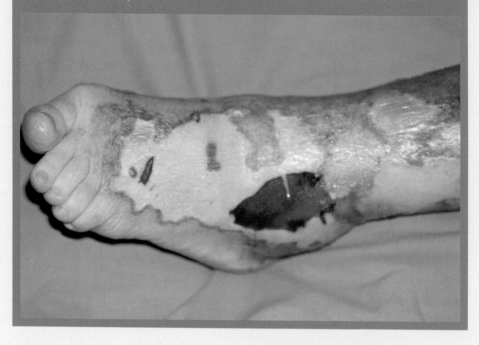

This patient's foot and leg are infected with a flesh-eating disease. The disease is caused by several bacteria that are resistant to antibiotics.

Fast Fact

When treating patients, modern doctors have more than 120 different antibiotics to choose from. And new antibiotics are being developed.

(basic chemical makeup), developing resistance to antibiotics that once killed them. Called super bugs, these new forms of germs shrug off (resist) big doses of antibiotics that once would have worked quickly. As germs

Scientists report the first form of staph infection that is resistant to penicillin.

1945

change, scientists must keep developing new kinds of antibiotics to fight them.

Lifesaving Medicines

How did antibiotics change the world? Antibiotics save lives. Before antibiotics, pneumonia, a lung disease, was the number one cause of death in the United States. About one-third of the people who got pneumonia died. Since the invention of antibiotics, most patients who get pneumonia recover.

Antibiotics also save money. Millions of people get infections each year. Before antibiotics, many people had to spend weeks in the hospital recovering from infections. Hospital stays are very expensive.

A BELLYFUL OF GERMS

Stomach ulcers are sores inside the stomach. They bleed and ache. Doctors once thought that stress and spicy foods caused ulcers. There was no cure. Some patients with ulcers had to stay in the hospital for long periods. They had to swallow nasty tasting medicine. Sometimes doctors had to operate to remove patients' ulcers. In 1986 scientists discovered that bacteria cause stomach ulcers. After this discovery, doctors began treating some people with ulcers with antibiotics instead of surgery and other medicines.

With the invention of antibiotics, most people can recover at home, taking antibiotics in pill form, usually for several days to several weeks.

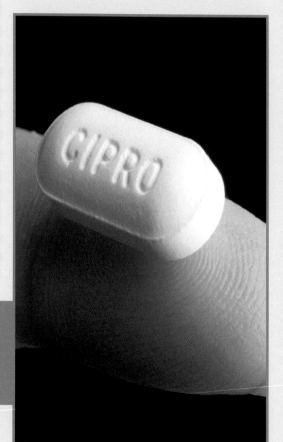

One of the latest generations of antibiotics, Cipro (ciprofloxacin hydrochloride) has worked well on antibiotic-resistant bacteria.

Scientists discover that bacteria cause stomach ulcers, which means ulcers can be treated with antibiotics.

1986

CHAPTER 4

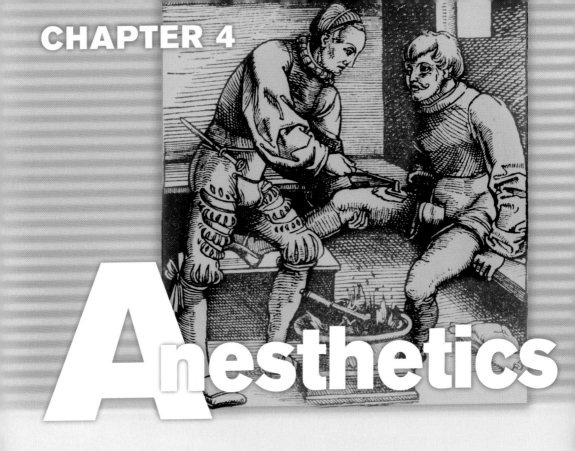

Anesthetics

In 1841 a man needed an operation for tongue cancer. With one stroke of a knife, Dr. John Collins Warren cut off the tip of the man's tongue. Then Dr. Warren touched a red-hot iron to the cut to stop the bleeding.

Wide awake, the patient felt it all. Wild with pain, he jumped up and ran away from the operating table. Dr. Warren's assistants caught him. Again, Dr. Warren administered the hot iron to stop the bleeding. As the man squirmed, the iron burned his lips, making the pain worse.

The man felt the whole operation because doctors then had no anesthetics—medicines to numb pain. No wonder patients dreaded having surgery.

Early Anesthetics

Before the mid-1800s, doctors had few effective treatments for pain. To ease the pain of surgery, some doctors punched patients in the jaw to knock them unconscious. Other doctors got patients drunk with whiskey or gave them dangerous drugs such as opium. These

DR. FAST, DR. FASTER, AND DR. FASTEST

Before anesthetics, the best surgeon was a fast surgeon. Since patients felt horrible pain during surgery, operations had to be done fast. Some surgeons boasted that they could cut off an arm in a minute. But even the best surgeons could not work fast enough to avoid inflicting pain. Patients would scream in agony. They had to be tied to the operating table or held down by strong men. Anesthetics put an end to all that suffering.

Alcohol vapor anesthesia, 1500s

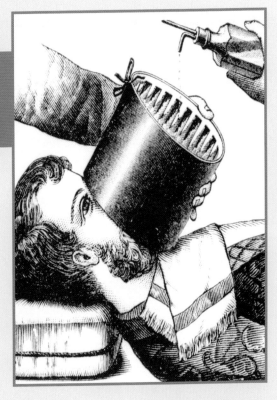

A patient inhales ether vapor prior to an operation in the 1800s.

treatments were only slightly effective in numbing the pain of surgery.

In 1799 the British scientist Humphry Davy experimented with a gas called nitrous oxide. He found that inhaling the gas relieved pain. Davy called nitrous oxide "laughing gas" because people got giggly after breathing it. In 1818 Michael Faraday, another British scientist, discovered that the vapor (fumes) of a liquid called ether had similar effects.

In 1842 Dr. Crawford Long, a Georgia physician, had a patient inhale ether vapors before surgery. The ether made the patient unconscious and insensitive to the pain of the surgery. But Dr. Long did not announce his discovery. Other doctors knew nothing about it.

Humphry Davy uses nitrous oxide ("laughing gas") to relieve pain during surgery.

1799

In 1844 Horace Wells, a Connecticut dentist, inhaled nitrous oxide himself before having a tooth pulled. He fell unconscious and felt no pain during the procedure. Unlike Dr. Long, Dr. Wells told other dentists and doctors about his experience.

The next doctor to use ether was William Morton, a Boston dentist. On October 18, 1846, Dr. Morton had a surgical patient inhale ether vapor. Then surgeons operated on the man in front of a big audience of doctors and medical students. The man slept peacefully as the surgeon cut into his neck. Amazing! The operation was painless.

> **BRAIN TEASER**
>
> Can pain be good for you? Actually, *some* pain is good. Pain can be a natural warning signal that something is wrong. It can alert you to take action to avoid more danger. For instance, pain can warn you: "That pot is hot! Take your finger away before you get a deep burn," or "Don't run on that sprained ankle. You'll hurt it more."

The news spread fast. Other doctors began using ether. It was not without problems, however. Patients often felt sick to their stomachs and vomited after awakening from ether anesthesia. Nevertheless, ether allowed doctors to perform operations slowly and carefully, never worried that their patients might feel pain.

The development of ether anesthesia led scientists to invent even better anesthetics. One of the most important was sodium pentothal. Two U.S. scientists, Ernest Volwiler and Donalee Tabern, developed this drug in 1936. Sodium pentothal was the

William Morton demonstrates the use of ether to a team of doctors and medical students.

1846

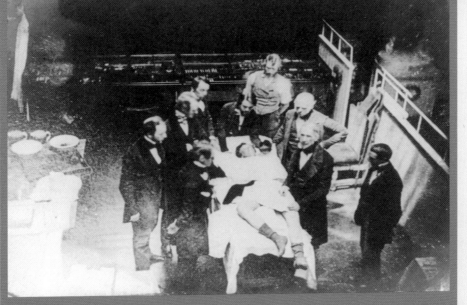

Dr. Morton *(second from top on the right)* and other medical staff reenact the successful use of ether anesthesia for surgery in 1850. Others had successfully used ether prior to Morton's demonstration in October 1846.

first anesthetic that could be injected into the body in liquid form. It worked fast. Patients fell asleep in seconds.

Zeroing in on Pain

Ether, nitrous oxide, and sodium pentothal are called general anesthetics. They put patients to sleep and block pain all over the body. Sometimes, however, doctors don't want to make patients unconscious during treatments. For instance, women having babies want to stay awake during the birthing process. So doctors often give women anesthetics that allow them to stay awake but block pain in the lower

ANCIENT WISDOM

In ancient times, doctors in Egypt, Greece, Rome, and other lands knew how to make painkilling drugs from plants. Some ancient Chinese doctors used a procedure called acupuncture to treat pain. They stuck thin needles into certain areas of the body, relieving pain in other parts of the body. Some modern doctors also use acupuncture to treat pain and other health problems.

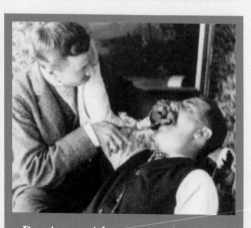

Dentistry without novocaine, 1890

parts of the body. Medicines that block pain in just one area are called local anesthetics.

Local anesthetics are less powerful than general anesthetics. They take less time to wear off, allowing patients to return to their regular lives sooner. One of the most commonly used local anesthetics is novocaine, invented by a German scientist, Alfred Einhorn, in 1905.

No More Ouch!

How has anesthesia changed people's lives? Think about getting a tooth filled—or pulled—before anesthetics were dis- covered. It hurt. There were no medicines to take away the pain of drilling or pulling teeth. Many people were afraid to go to the dentist. Their teeth rotted and ached, but they still didn't get treatment. By the

Alfred Einhorn invents
novocaine, a common
local anesthetic.

1905

A girl about to receive novocaine. Though she may feel some pain from the needle, the drug will keep her pain free during the dental procedure.

age of thirty, many people had lost all their teeth.

Then think about going to the dentist for a filling in modern times. The dentist first puts a liquid anesthetic on your gums (the pink tissue surrounding your teeth). This anesthetic keeps you from fully feeling the pain from a shot of local anesthetic. This shot numbs your tooth, so the dentist can drill out the tooth decay painlessly.

U.S. scientists develop sodium pentothal, the first anesthetic that can be injected in liquid form.

1936

CHAPTER 5

X-rays

Suppose you banged into another player during a soccer game. Doctors might want to see if you had a broken leg. They would use one of the most amazing medical inventions of all. It is the X-ray.

Few other medical inventions can do so much. X-rays can diagnose broken bones, cancer, and many other health problems. Doctors also use X-rays as a treatment. For instance, X-rays can slow or stop the growth of cancer cells.

X-rays can't be seen with the human eye. Nobody can feel them with a fingertip. X-rays are pure energy. They are like light, radio waves, and the microwaves that pop popcorn.

Is That Screen *Glowing*?

A German scientist named Wilhelm Roentgen discovered X-rays in 1895. He was studying radiation, a kind of energy, given off by a cathode-ray tube (similar to an old-fashioned TV picture tube).

Roentgen turned the tube on. Then he glanced at a glass screen a few feet away. The screen was glowing. He turned the tube off. The glow disappeared. He turned it back on. Hello, glow. The tube was giving off invisible rays! They passed through the air and made the screen's surface glow. Roentgen didn't know what they were. He named them X-rays.

William Roentgen

The Bones in Bertha's Hand

Next, Roentgen's hand accidentally got in the way of the X-ray beam. His jaw dropped when he saw the screen. Glowing there was an image of the bones inside his hand. Roentgen had discovered that X-rays pass through human flesh, but not bone. That's why the bones left an image, like a shadow, on the screen.

Roentgen asked his wife, Bertha, to put her hand on photographic film. Then he exposed her hand to X-rays. When the film was developed, it showed an image of the bones in Bertha's hand. That photograph was the first X-ray picture. News about X-rays spread like wildfire. Doctors around the world began using X-rays to see inside the body.

A Window on the Body

X-rays allow doctors to see inside the body—literally. An X-ray of a

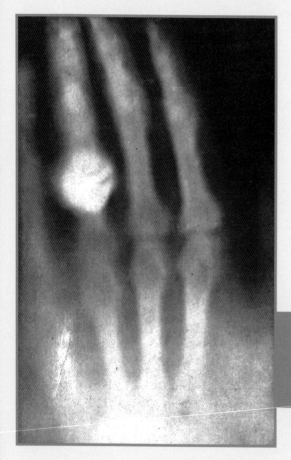

Roentgen's first X-ray of his wife Bertha's hand. Bertha's hand bones and wedding rings are visible.

Wilhelm Roentgen makes an X-ray of his wife's hand. The picture shows her bones and wedding ring.

1895

Wilhelm Roentgen receives the first Nobel Prize in Physics.

1901

broken bone helps doctors figure out the best way to set it. X-rays of the chest tell doctors whether people have serious lung diseases such as tuberculosis or lung cancer. X-rays help doctors spot cancer and other life-threatening diseases early—often before a person has any symptoms, or outward signs, of disease. By catching diseases early, X-rays help doctors save thousands of lives each year.

X-rays also make surgery simpler. Before X-rays, surgeons often had to guess about where to make their incisions. If they needed to remove a bullet, they simply cut and cut until they found it. But with X-rays, surgeons can see the exact location of diseased tissue, bones, and foreign objects, such as bullets. X-rays enable doctors to make their incisions at exactly the right place.

X-rays help dentists too. By X-raying patients' teeth, dentists can find tooth decay in spots that are hard to see with just the eye. Dentists can also tell if the roots of a patient's teeth are healthy.

X-Ray Vision

After Wilhelm Roentgen discovered X-rays, people got excited by the mysterious new rays. Writers began putting X-rays into their comic books, television shows, and movies. For instance, Superman, the famous comic book character, was said to have X-ray vision. He could see right through walls. In some stories, X-rays turned people and animals into monsters. None of these stories about X-rays were scientifically accurate, however.

PET X-Rays

PET scanning, or positron emission tomography, is a kind of computerized X-ray process. Other X-rays show only how the body looks inside. PET scans show how chemicals are acting inside the brain and other organs. Different kinds of chemical activity show up as different colors on a PET scan. By studying PET scans, doctors can tell if the brain or another organ is working properly.

Better X-Rays

The first X-rays weren't perfect. For example, they could not make clear pictures of soft, non-bony parts of the body, such as the heart, the stomach, and other organs. Then scientists invented special dyes that show up on X-rays. Other scientists invented ways to inject the dyes into the body. These dyes made soft structures show up clearly on X-rays.

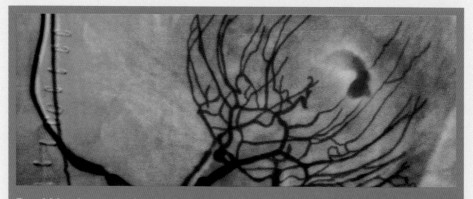

Dyed blood vessels clearly show up in this X-ray of a human stomach. Dyes help doctors X-ray soft tissues. Here, bleeding shows up as a red stain.

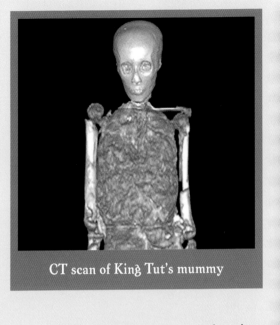

CT scan of King Tut's mummy

Oh, Mummy!

X-rays are not just for doctors. They also let scientists see inside mummies from ancient Egypt and other lands. Mummies are dead bodies that have been preserved with fluids and then wrapped in layers of cloth. Scientists who study mummies don't want to cut into them and destroy them. Instead, they use X-rays to make pictures of the mummies' bones and bodies without doing any damage. X-rays of Egyptian mummies have revealed health problems, such as tooth decay and broken bones.

CT scanning was another important invention. CT stands for computed tomography. Regular X-rays look flat, like the pictures in a book. CT scanners turn regular X-rays into lifelike, three-dimensional pictures. Allan Cormack of the United States and Godfrey Hounsfield of Great Britain invented CT scanning in 1972.

Although they can save lives, X-rays can also be dangerous. Exposure to too many X-rays can cause cancer and other health problems. When needed to help a sick person, however, X-rays are often worth the risk. Doctors use X-rays only when they are needed.

Allan Cormack and Godfrey Hounsfield invent CT scanning.
1972

CHAPTER 6

Artificial Limbs

Captain Hook, the pirate in *Peter Pan* (a play and novel), had a steel hook instead of a hand. Long John Silver, a pirate in the book *Treasure Island*, walked on a wooden leg. Artificial (human-made) limbs like those described in the books were really used in the past. They were not fancy. They did not work very well. Nevertheless, they enabled people without their own limbs to work and play.

Millions of people have artificial limbs. Some were born without arms or legs or with limbs that didn't work right. Others lost limbs in accidents or wars. Still others had diseases that could be treated only by amputation (cutting off an arm or leg). Losing a limb makes it hard to do the simplest things: just try dressing yourself with one hand. But people who have lost limbs can live quite well, thanks to prosthetic (artificial) limbs.

Modern prosthetic limbs can do more than just snare things, like Captain Hook's hook hand. They can do more than just support a person's weight, like Long John Silver's wooden leg. Modern artificial limbs work like natural limbs. The fingers on an artificial hand, for example, can pick up objects. The knees and ankles on artificial legs can flex and turn just like real body parts. Modern artificial limbs are lightweight, strong, and comfortable to use. They look natural, much like real arms and legs.

> ## FAST FACT
> About three million people in the United States are amputees (people who have had a limb amputated).

He Cut Off His Foot

Nobody knows when the first artificial limb was made. An ancient Greek historian, Herodotus, wrote about one early artificial limb about 500 B.C. Herodotus told about a prisoner who escaped from chains by cutting off his own foot. He later walked with a wooden foot. In 1858 archaeologists dug up the oldest artificial limb ever found. It was a leg made of copper and wood, dating to about 300 B.C.

Archaeologists find an artificial
leg dating to about 300 B.C.
1858

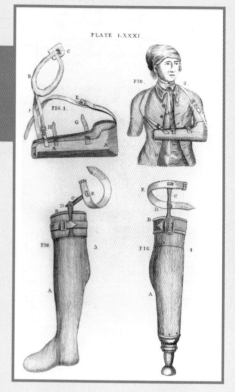

This illustration from the 1700s shows wooden arms and wooden legs. Early artificial limbs were heavy and hard to use.

Some early artificial legs were made of a leather cup attached to a wooden peg. The cup fit over the stump—the remaining portion of the wearer's leg. Straps attached the cup to the wearer's body. Artificial arms and hands were made the same way.

The first artificial limbs were stiff and did not have joints that bent like real arms, hands, and legs. The limbs were also heavy and uncomfortable. People could wear them for only short periods. Moreover, the straps often came undone, and the limbs fell off.

Better Artificial Limbs

Ambroise Pare, a French surgeon, invented movable artificial limbs around 1580. One was a hand operated by springs, which pulled the fingers tight around objects. Another was a leg with a movable knee joint. In 1863 Dubois Parmelee of New York City invented a way to attach artificial limbs to the body using suction, a sort of vacuum action. Limbs attached with suction stayed on better and were more comfortable than those attached by straps.

Wars created a need for even better artificial limbs. During the U.S. Civil War (1861–1865) and World War I (1914–1918), thousands of wounded soldiers had to have arms or legs amputated. To help these soldiers, inventors began to build artificial limbs from stronger, lighter materials.

Phantom Limbs

For a while after an amputation, people may feel pain and other feelings in the part of the body that's no longer there. Doctors call this sensation phantom limb pain. It happens because the brain does not yet realize that part of the body is gone.

By the mid-1900s, designers were making artificial limbs from superstrong plastics and metals like those used in spacecraft. Designers used electronics and computers to make artificial limbs work even better.

High-Tech Arms and Legs

In the 1960s, inventors figured out how to make artificial limbs controlled by myoelectricity—the electricity produced inside human muscles. These artificial limbs have sensors that pick up

Dubois Parmelee devises
a way to attach artificial
limbs using suction.

1863

electrical signals from the wearer's body. For instance, a wearer might flex a shoulder muscle, sending electrical signals to a motor in an artificial hand. The motor then makes the hand's fingers pinch.

One of the most famous artificial limbs is the Utah Arm, created in 1981 at the University of Utah. The Utah Arm is made from electronic and mechanical parts, all powered by a rechargeable battery. The arm's elbow, wrist, and fingers all move like natural body parts. With this arm, the wearer can pick up a raw egg and hold it securely, but not so tightly that the eggshell cracks.

In 2003 doctors at the Rehabilitation Institute of Chicago made another great advance in artificial limbs. They developed a prosthetic arm that could be controlled by a

Wearing a Utah Arm *(right arm)*, a mother plays with her baby. The bionic limb looks and works almost like a natural limb.

Scientists at the University of Utah create the lifelike Utah Arm.

1981

patient's thoughts. The arm takes advantage of the electrical connections that already exist in the human nervous system. When the wearer thinks about bending the arm, the brain sends an electrical signal through the nerves to electrical devices in the arm.

Living without Limbs

Thanks to artificial limbs, people who lose a limb can still have full, active lives. How active? In 1999 Ed Hommer climbed Alaska's Mount McKinley, the highest mountain in North America, on two artificial legs. In 2003 Aron Ralston had to amputate his own arm when it got pinned under a boulder during a solo wilderness hike. Even with only one arm, Ralston didn't want to give up hiking, mountain climbing, and other outdoor sports. So designers made him a special artificial arm with a mountain climber's pick in place of a hand.

CYBORGS

In the 1970s, *The Six Million Dollar Man* and *The Bionic Woman* TV shows featured humans with artificial body parts. Because of their mechanical body parts, these characters had superhuman powers. Newer movies, TV shows, and computer games feature characters called cyborgs. They, too, are part human and part machine.

Doctors at the Rehabilitation Institute of Chicago create an artificial limb that can be controlled by the wearer's thoughts.

2003

Epilogue

Cathy cut her foot on a sharp piece of glass at the beach. It became infected. She needed crutches to help her walk. Did she need an antibiotic, a medicine to treat the infection? No way! Not in 2010!

Instead, the doctor called in the robots—100 billion zillion robots. The doctor gave Cathy a shot in the arm. It put billions of "nanomachines" into her blood.

Anything called "nano" is very, very small. One nanosecond is a billionth of a second, for instance. The robots the doctor used to treat Cathy in the fictional scenario above were so small that four-hundred of them would fit across a human hair. The nanomachines had microscopic gears, linkages, and wheels, just like big machines.

When the tiny machines reached the infection, some of them attacked the bacteria that were making Cathy sick. Others repaired damage caused by the bacteria. She could walk normally again.

Nanotechnology is just one of many new technologies that will help doctors prevent, diagnose, and treat diseases in the future. Some nanomachines may be robot surgeons, with spinning blades to clear away fatty deposits blocking an artery, for instance. Other nanomachines might have tiny sensors, almost like microscopic smoke detectors. The machines will attach to cells inside the body. When a disease starts, the sensors will send a signal. Doctors will be able to treat the disease before it spreads and gets worse. Some nanomachines will attach to and destroy cancer cells. Others will act like pills that deliver medicine only to diseased parts of the body. Nanomachines will be injected with a shot. They will repair diseased organs from the inside, without any pain or cutting into the skin. People in the future will benefit from amazing bionic body parts. Bionics is the use of electronic devices and machines to replace parts of the human body. Bionic artificial limbs will become more natural. People will even use their thoughts to make an artificial leg or arm move. People with disabilities will benefit from bionic eyes, ears, and other body parts. These electronic devices will connect to nerves in the body. They will work almost like natural organs.

Someday, scientists hope that bionic artificial limbs won't even be necessary. Instead, scientists want to grow new body parts to replace those damaged by accidents or disease. Genetic engineering may make it possible. Genes are substances that control how the body works and grows. Scientists already know how to engineer (change and design) genes to grow new skin and other body tissue. In the future, scientists may discover how to grow whole limbs.

Some future medical inventions sound far-fetched. Imagine transplanting a human head onto a different person's body. Imagine pills that make people smarter, or hearts grown in a laboratory for transplants. Imagine giving people a gene that lets them eat without getting fat or live to age 125. Such ideas may sound like science fiction, but scientists already are at work on them.

1674 Anton van Leeuwenhoek is the first person to see germs, or microorganisms, through a microscope.

1796 Edward Jenner invents the first vaccine. It protects James Phipps from smallpox.

1799 Humphry Davy discovers that inhaling nitrous oxide (laughing gas) relieves pain.

1818 Michael Faraday discovers that inhaled ether vapor relieves pain.

1844 Ignaz Semmelweis discovers that hand washing prevents the spread of disease. Horace Wells uses nitrous oxide to prevent pain during the pulling of teeth.

1846 William Morton gives ether to a patient to prevent pain during surgery.

1863 Dubois Parmelee experiments with attaching artificial limbs to the body by suction.

1865 Joseph Lister develops an antiseptic spray to kill germs.

1882 Robert Koch proves that the tuberculosis (TB) germ causes TB.

1885 Louis Pasteur invents a rabies vaccine.

1895 Wilhelm Roentgen discovers X-rays.

1905 Alfred Einhorn invents a local anesthetic called novocaine.

1921 The first tuberculosis vaccine is invented.

1928 Alexander Fleming discovers penicillin.

1936 Ernest Volwiler and Donalee Tabern invent sodium pentothal.

1941 Scientists develop a way to make penicillin in large amounts.

1943 Selman Waksman discovers streptomycin, the first antibiotic for treating TB.

1954 Jonas Salk creates the first polio vaccine.

1957 Albert Sabin creates the second polio vaccine.

1963 The vaccine for common measles goes into use.

1972 Allan Cormack and Godfrey Hounsfield invent computed tomography (CT scans).

1981 The Utah Arm, a myoelectric artificial arm, is invented at the University of Utah.

1986 The germs that cause stomach ulcers are discovered.

1998 Doctors in the United States write 80 million prescriptions for antibiotics—25 million pounds (11.3 kilograms) of medicine.

1999 Ed Hommer climbs Mount McKinley on two artificial legs.

2003 Doctors at the Rehabilitation Institute of Chicago develop a bionic arm that can be controlled by a patient's thoughts.

2005 Advances in nanotechnology improve building materials, clothing, and consumer products. Research in nanotechnology continues with the possible future development of nanobots.

GLOSSARY

amputees: people who have had a limb or limbs amputated

anesthetics: substances that cause a loss of pain or other feeling. Some anesthetics cause people to lose consciousness.

antibiotics: chemicals that stop bacteria from growing inside the body

antiseptic: a liquid or other substance that kills germs

bacteria: microorganisms found in living things, soil, water, and other substances. Some bacteria cause disease.

genetic engineering: altering the genes, or basic chemical makeup, of a living thing

germs: microorganisms that cause disease

immunity: protection from or resistance to a certain disease

infected: filled with germs or disease

microorganism: a tiny living thing, such as a bacteria. Some microorganisms can cause disease.

prosthesis: an artificial limb

public health departments: agencies that try to improve the health of people in communities using education, sanitation, medicine, and other efforts

vaccine: a preparation, often administered with a shot, that gives a person immunity, or resistance, to a certain disease

viruses: microorganisms that live inside another living thing. Viruses often cause disease.

SELECTED BIBLIOGRAPHY

Adler, Robert E. *Medical Firsts: From Hippocrates to the Human Genome.* New York: John Wiley & Sons, 2004.

Darling, David. *Beyond 2000: The Health Revolution, Surgery and Medicine in the Twenty-First Century.* Parsippany, NJ: Dillon Press, 1996.

Harrison, Peter. *All about Inventions: Amazing Breakthroughs That Shaped Our World.* London: Anness Publishing, Ltd, 2000.

Ingpen, Robert R. *Encyclopedia of Ideas That Changed the World: The Greatest Discoveries and Inventions of Human History.* Surrey, UK: Dragon's World, 1993.

Jeffrey, Kirk. *Machines in Our Hearts: The Cardiac Pacemaker, the Implantable Defibrillator, and American Health Care.* Baltimore: Johns Hopkins University Press, 2001.

Leikin, Jerrold B. *American Medical Association Complete Medical Encyclopedia.* New York: Random House Reference, 2003.

McGrew, Roderick E. *Encyclopedia of Medical History.* New York: McGraw-Hill, 1985.

Null, Gary. *Germs, Biological Warfare, Vaccinations: What You Need to Know.* New York: Seven Stories Press, 2003.

Porter, Roy. *Blood and Guts: A Short History of Medicine.* New York: Norton, 2002.

FURTHER READING AND WEBSITES

Alphin, Elaine Marie. *Germ Hunter: A Story about Louis Pasteur.* Minneapolis: Carolrhoda Books Inc., 2003.
This biography examines the life of the famous scientist, whose investigations into germs ultimately saved countless lives.

Dr. Jonas Salk
http://www.wic.org/bio/jsalk.htm
At this site created by the Women's International Center, visitors can learn about Jonas Salk and the polio vaccine.

Fridell, Ron. *Decoding Life: Unraveling the Mysteries of the Genome.* Minneapolis: Lerner Publications Company, 2005.
Learn about DNA, the genetic blueprint for all life, the study of the genome, and how discoveries benefit medicine.

Gherman, Beverly. *The Mysterious Rays of Dr. Roentgen.* New York: Atheneum/Macmillan, 1994.
This book examines Wilhelm Roentgen's discovery of X-rays and later discoveries that revealed the ill effects of the mysterious rays.

Gottfried, Ted. *Alexander Fleming: Discoverer of Penicillin.* New York: Franklin Watts, 1997.
Alexander Fleming's discovery was only the first step in making penicillin available to patients, as this wonderful resource discusses.

History of Prostheses
http://www.uihealthcare.com/depts/medmuseum/wallexhibits/body/histofpros/histofpros.html
Created by the University of Iowa Medical Museum, this site provides a history of prosthetic devices and interesting drawings of artificial limbs.

Just for Kids
http://www.nsf.gov/od/lpa/events/justforkids.htm
This site from the Office of Legislative Public Affairs contains questions that students have asked scientists, plus games and excellent links.

Louis Pasteur (1822–1895)
http://www.accessexcellence.com/AB/BC/Louis_Pasteur.html
This site from the National Health Museum is a good resource on Louis Pasteur, with links to a resource center, activities, and further information.

McPherson, Stephanie Sammartino. *Jonas Salk: Conquering Polio.* Minneapolis: Lerner Publications Company, 2002.
This book offers a good biography of polio vaccine pioneer Jonas Salk, as well as information about the nature of scientific theory and discovery.

Naden, Corinne J., and Rose Blue. *Jonas Salk: Polio Pioneer.* Brookfield, CT: Millbrook Press, 2001.
This well-written biography examines the life of Jonas Salk and his creation of the breakthrough polio vaccine. Photographs, sidebars, and fact boxes add to the narrative.

Science News for Kids
http://www.sciencenewsforkids.org/
This site is an excellent source of current science news, with information on infectious diseases, X-rays, and artificial limbs.

Seiple, Samantha, and Todd Seiple. *Mutants, Clones, and Killer Corn.* Minneapolis: Lerner Publications Company, 2005.
This volume is a good guide for learning more about genetic engineering, including its uses in fighting diseases, modifying crops, and growing tissues.

Skurzynski, Gloria. *Waves: The Electromagnetic Universe*. Washington, DC: National Geographic Society, 1996.
    The author provides clear, simple explanations of the electromagnetic spectrum, which includes X-rays.

Smith, Linda Wasmer. *Louis Pasteur, Disease Fighter*. Springfield, NJ: Enslow Publishers, 1997.
    This biography explains Pasteur's discoveries and describes the great scientist's world.

Waxman, Laura Hamilton. *Marie Curie*. Minneapolis: Lerner Publications Company, 2004.
    During World War I, Curie, a Nobel Prize—winning scientist, transported X-ray equipment to army hospitals. Her efforts helped save the lives of thousands of soldiers. This book tells her story.

"What's Good about Sewer Bacteria? More Than You Think."
    http://www.ars.usda.gov/is/kids/weirdscience/story1/bacteriaframe.htm
    Created by the U.S. Department of Agriculture, this web page offers interesting information about bacteria, especially bacteria found in sewers.

Wise, William. *Nell of Branford Hall*. New York: Dial Books, 1999.
    This historical novel features a girl named Nell, who lives in a village struck by the plague of 1665. The book gives readers a firsthand account of life before antibiotics or vaccines.

Woods, Michael, and Mary B. Woods. *Ancient Medicine: From Sorcery to Surgery*. Minneapolis: Runestone Press, 2000.
    Discover more information about the history of medicine in this engaging and entertaining book.

INDEX

acupuncture, 30

amputate, amputation, amputee(s), 39, 41, 43

anesthesia, 28, 30. *See also* anesthesic(s)

anesthetic(s), 25, 26, 27, 29–30: general, 29; liquid, 28, 29, 31; local, 29–30. *See also* ether anesthesia; novocaine; sodium pentothol

anthrax, 15

antibiotic(s), 18-24, 44, 46, 47: mass production of, 24; resistance to, 21-22. *See also* mold; Penicillium notatum

antiseptic, 10–11

bacteria, 7, 8, 10, 18–20, 22, 24, 44

Bertha's hand, 33–34

bionics, 45: bionic limb, 42, 45, 47

bleeding and blood, 6, 25: blood vessels, 36

body, 12, 14, 18, 29, 30, 34, 35, 36, 39–43, 45

bones, 33–34, 35: broken, 32

brain, 36

cancer, 32, 37, 45: cancer, lung, 35

cathode-ray tube, 33

chemicals, 18, 21

children, 16, 17, 18

cholera, 15

cleanliness, 6–11

computed tomography (CT), 37

computers, 36, 41, 43

Cormack, Allan, 37

cure, 5, 21, 24

cyborgs, 43

Davy, Humphry, 27

dentist(s), 11, 28, 30, 31, 35

design and designers, 41, 43

disease(s), 6, 7, 8, 9, 10, 12, 13, 16, 17, 18, 19, 20, 22, 23, 35, 39; causes of: damp air, 8; evil spirits, 19; germ theory of, 9, 10, 11

doctor(s), 5, 6, 7, 8, 10, 11, 17, 20, 21, 24, 26–29, 34–35, 32, 36, 41, 42–43, 44, 45, 47

drug(s), 19–20, 21, 28–29: opium, 26; painkilling, 5, 30. *See also* anesthetic(s); miracle drugs

Einhorn, Alfred, 30

electronics, 41–42: electronic parts, 42

ether anesthesia, 27, 28, 29

Faraday, Michael, 27

Fleming, Alexander, 19

flesh-eating disease, 22

foreign objects, 35

fungus, 19

genes, 17

genetic form, 21

genetically engineered plants, 17

germ(s), 5, 6, 7, 8, 9, 12, 14, 19, 20, 21, 22

government agencies, 8, 9

hand washing, 6, 7, 8, 10, 11
healthcare professionals, 11
heart, 36, 45
Herodotus, 39
hiking, 43
Hommer, Ed, 43
hospitals, 8, 23
Hounsfield, Godfrey, 37
human waste, 7, 9
hygiene, 9

illness, 7, 19, 21
immunity, 12–14
infection, 6, 7, 18, 19–22, 23:
  of ear, 18; infected wounds,
  20–21, 44
influenza (the flu), 17
injection, 14, 15, 17
injury, 19, 21, 41, 43, 44
invention(s), 5, 7, 10, 15, 23, 24, 40,
  41, 45

Jenner, Edward, 13, 14, 15

knives, 5, 25
Koch, Robert, 10, 46

laboratory, 19, 21, 46
laughing gas. See nitrous oxide
Leeuwenhoek, Anton van, 8, 46
limbs, artificial, 38–43, 45, 47;
  control of, 39, 41–43; oldest ever
  found, 39; phantom, 41; Utah Arm,
  42, 47

limbs, prosthetic (artificial). See limbs,
  artificial
Lister, Joseph, 10, 46
Long, Crawford, 27, 28

maternity ward, 8
measles, 17, 46
mechanical parts, 42
medical: discoveries, 7; inventions, 5;
  staff, 29; students, 11, 28
medicine(s), 18–19, 24, 26, 30
microorganisms, 7. See also bacteria;
  germs; viruses
milkmaid(s), 12, 13
miracle drugs, 5, 18–19
mold, 5, 19–20, 21. See also
  antibiotic(s); Penicillium notatum
Morton, William, 28, 29, 46
Mount McKinley, 43, 47
mumps, 17
myoelectricity, 41–42

nitrous oxide, 27, 28, 29, 46
novocaine, 30, 46

operating: rooms, 10–11; table,
  25
operation(s), 5, 25–26, 28
organs, 36, 45, 46

pain, 5, 25–27, 28, 29–30, 31, 41
Pare, Ambroise, 40
Parmelee, Dubois, 41, 46
Pasteur, Louis, 9, 10, 46

patient(s), 11, 26, 27, 28
peg (wooden) legs, 38, 39–40, 40.
   See also limbs, artificial
Penicillium notatum (penicillin),
   19–20, 21, 46
PET scan. *See* positron emission
   tomography
Phipps, James, 13, 14, 46
pneumonia, 20, 23
polio, 16–17, 46. *See also* Salk, Jonas
positron emission tomography (PET
   scanning), 36
prevention, 7, 15, 16–17
prosthetics, 39, 42–43. *See also* limbs,
   artificial
puerperal fever, 8. *See also* hand
   washing; infection
pus, 6, 12–14. *See also* infection

radiation, 33
Ralston, Aron, 43
Roentgen, Wilhelm, 33–34, 35, 46
Roosevelt, Franklin D., 16

Sabin, Albert, 16, 46
Salk, Jonas, 16, 46: and polio vaccine,
   16–17. *See also* vaccination(s) and
   vaccine(s)
scarlet fever, 20
scientist(s), 5, 7, 9, 10, 12, 13, 15, 16,
   17, 19, 21, 24, 27, 28, 30, 33, 36,
   45, 46
Semmelweis, Ignaz, 8, 9, 46
side effects, 21, 28

smallpox, 12–15, 17
sodium pentothol, 28–29, 46
staphylococcus bacteria (staph), 7,
   19, 20
sterilize, 11
stomach, 24, 36: ulcers, 24, 47. *See
   also* bacteria
streptomycin, 21, 46. *See also*
   antibiotic(s)
super bugs, 21, 22
surgeon(s), 10, 26, 27, 28–29, 35, 40
surgery, 10, 11, 24, 26, 27, 28–29, 35

Tabern, Donalee, 28, 46
teeth and tooth decay, 31, 35
tuberculosis (TB), 15, 21, 35

U.S. Centers for Disease Control and
   Prevention (CDC), 8, 16

vaccination(s) and vaccine(s), 12–14,
   15, 16–17, 46
virus(es), 7, 12, 16, 17, 20
Volwiler, Ernest, 28

Waksman, Selman, 21, 46
Warren, John Collins, 25
wars, 41: U.S. Civil War, 41; World
   War I, 41; World War II, 20, 21
Wells, Horace, 28, 46
whooping cough, 17

X-rays, 32–37, 46: dangers of, 37;
   x-ray vision, 35

COVER AND CHAPTER OPENER PHOTO CAPTIONS

cover Top: A man receives surgery on his arm without anesthesia in the 1600s. Bottom: Surgeons operate on a fully anesthetized patient during the 2000s.

pp. 4–5 A surgeon operates on a patient during the late 1400s.

p. 6 This illustration shows an operation in progress during the 1800s. The patient is held down because the operation takes place without anesthesia.

p. 12 Nurses tend to smallpox sufferers in Great Britain during the early 1800s.

p. 18 Penicillin *(center)* stops the growth of pneumonia virus *(clear area around the penicillin)* in a petri dish.

p. 25 A patient withstands the agonizing pain of cauterization (burning a wound shut) without anesthesia in the 1600s.

p. 32 A boy lies on an X-ray table in 1915. X-ray machines allow doctors to look inside the body without cutting.

p. 38 This 1750 illustration shows assistants restraining a man while a doctor saws off the man's diseased arm.

pp. 44–45 Medical nanobots make their way through the human blood stream to fight disease in this artist's illustration of the theoretical machines.

ABOUT THE AUTHORS
Michael Woods is a science and medical journalist who has won many national writing awards. He works in the National Bureau of the *Pittsburgh Post-Gazette* and *Toledo Blade* newspapers. Mary B. Woods has worked as a librarian in the Fairfax County Public School System in Virginia and at the Benjamin Franklin International School in Barcelona, Spain. The Woodses' previous books include the eight-volume Ancient Technology series. The Woodses have four children and two grandchildren.